I0119872

William H. Browne

Pennsylvania Legal Time-Table

Condensed From Acts of Assembly & Rules of Courts in Pennsylvania

William H. Browne

Pennsylvania Legal Time-Table
Condensed From Acts of Assembly & Rules of Courts in Pennsylvania

ISBN/EAN: 9783337158842

Printed in Europe, USA, Canada, Australia, Japan

Cover: Foto ©Suzi / pixelio.de

More available books at **www.hansebooks.com**

C.C. McGlaughlin

Musician,

Compliments of:

Cummins Fiske

April 1876

Legal Time-Table.

Condensed from Acts of Assembly and Rules of Courts in Pennsylvania.

BY

WILLIAM HARDCASTLE BROWNE, Esq.,

OF THE PHILADELPHIA BAR,

AUTHOR OF "DIGEST OF DIVORCE AND ALIMONY," ETC.

PHILADELPHIA:

KAY & BROTHER,

LAW BOOKSELLERS, PUBLISHERS AND IMPORTERS,

17 AND 19 SOUTH SIXTH STREET, EAST SIDE.

1875.

Entered according to Act of Congress, in the year 1875, by

WM. H. BROWNE,

In the Office of the Librarian of Congress, at Washington.

WESTCOTT & THOMSON,
Stereotypers and Electrotypers, Philada.

COLLINS, PRINTER.
Philada.

CONTENTS.

4 CONTENTS.

ADVERTISEMENTS APPLICABLE TO PHILADELPHIA.

Date of Act.		Legal Intelligencer. Number of Insertions.	Other papers.
1874, Feb. 12.	Act of Assembly—Notice of Application for Local and Special Legislation......	2	papers, 4 weeks once a week.
1857, May 13.	" " Notice of Application for Legislation affecting Real Estate.	1	paper, 6 publications.
1860, April 2.	" " Notice of Application for Incorporation......	2	papers, 1 publication.
1851, Oct. 14.	Appraisement—Widow's Claim. Orphans' Court. Rule IV......	1	paper, 2 weeks twice a week.
1836, June 14.	Assignee's Account—Notice of Filing. Common Pleas. Rule V......	2	papers, 4 weeks once a week.
1836, June 13.	Attachment of Vessels—Common Pleas Notice......	1	paper, 6 weeks once a week.
1846, April 20.	Auditor's Notice of Meeting, as to proceeds of Sheriff's Sales, and Accounts of Assignees and Trustees. Common Pleas. Rule VIII......	1	paper, 5 alternate days.
1832, Mar. 29. 1840, April 13.	{ Auditor's Notice of Meeting. Orphans' Court. Rule XIII......	1	paper, 5 alternate days.
1875, Mar. 18.	Audit Lists—Notice of Hearing. Orphans' Court. Rule II.......	3	papers, 2 times each.
1863, Dec. 14.	Carriers and Commission Men—Notice of Sale for Lien.......	1	paper, 3 weeks.
1832, Mar. 29.	Citation to Absent Party in Orphans' Court.......		Legal Intelligencer and 2 daily papers, at option of Court as to number of insertions.
1849, April 10.	Col. In. Tax. Register's Citation to Absent Executors and Heirs.......	4	1 paper, 4 weeks once a week.
1840, Oct. 13.	Corporations—Applications for Charter.......	3	1 paper, 3 weeks.
"	Applications for Dissolution.......	1	2 papers, 1 insertion.
"	Process against Home Corporations with office and officers elsewhere.......	6	1 paper, 6 weeks.

ADVERTISEMENTS APPLICABLE TO PHILADELPHIA—(CONTINUED).

Date of Act.			Legal Intelligencer, Number of Insertions.	Other papers.
1840, Oct. 13.	Corporations—Actions against non-resident Stockholders—Notice of Suit.....		4	1 paper, 4 times.
1874, April 29.	"	Applications for Charter, where not for profit.....	3	2 papers, 3 weeks once a week.
"	"	Applications for Charter, where for profit.....	2	2 papers, 3 weeks once a week.
"	"	Meeting to issue Preferred Stock.....	1	1 paper, 30 days.
"	"	Meeting to increase Capital Stock or indebtedness.....	1	1 paper, 60 days, once a week.
1832, Mar. 29. } 1851, April 3. }	Decedents' Estates—Orphans' Court. Notice to Absent Heirs, Legatees, etc., when required.....			Legal Intelligencer and daily papers, at option of Court as to number of insertions.
1834, Feb. 24.	"	" Common Pleas Notice to Absent Heirs, Legatees, etc., when required. Rule XXI.....	2	1 paper, 2 weeks twice a week.
1786, Mar. 23.	Deed—Lost or Illegible—Notice of Petition.....		3	1 paper, 3 weeks once a week.
1815, Mar. 13.	Divorce—Order of Publication by Sheriff.....		4	1 paper, once a week 4 weeks.
"	Common Pleas, Rule XVI. Notice of Interrogatories and Meeting, where Writ Served, and no Service of Interrogatories.....		2	1 paper, 15 times.
"	Rule XVI. Rule for a Decree, where Resp. not Personally Served		2	2 papers, 2 weeks twice a week.
1851, April 14.	Ejectment—Unoccupied Land, Notice of Suit for Specific Performance.....		3	1 paper, 3 insertions, over 60 days before return day.
1824, Mar. 29.	" Unoccupied Land, Sold for Taxes, Rule to Plead.....		9	1 paper, 60 days successively.
1787, Sept. 29.	Escheat—Notice of Sale of Lands.....		2	2 papers 1 month.

ADVERTISEMENTS APPLICABLE TO PHILADELPHIA—(CONTINUED).

Date of Act.		Legal Intelligencer. Number of Insertions.	Other papers.
1834, Feb. 24.	Executors and Administrators, Publication of Letters Testamentary and Administration................	6	1 paper, 6 weeks once a week.
1859, April 6.	Executors or administrators of deceased Plaintiff or Defendant; Publication of Scire Facias................	1	1 or more papers, at option of Court.
1836, June 13.	Foreign Attachment; Notice of Writ; affecting Vacant Real Estate........	6	1 paper, 6 weeks.
1840, April 8.	Ground Rent; Alias Writ Covenant. Rule XXXI	2	1 paper, 2 weeks once a week.
1836, June 16.	Insolvency—Notice of Hearing to Creditors. Rule XIX................	2	2 papers, 2 weeks 3 times a week.
"	Notice by Trustee of Appointment................	4	1 paper, 4 weeks.
1823, Mar. 31.	Mortgage—Notice to Absence or Defunct Corporation to Satisfy............	4	1 paper, 4 weeks once a week.
1862, Mar. 27.	" Forged,—Notice to Absent Mortgagee	8	2 papers, 8 weeks once a week.
1849, April 10.	" Lost................	4	1 paper, 4 weeks once a week.
1846, Mar. 11.	Municipal Claims; Synopsis of Scire Facias................	1	1 paper, 2 weeks twice a week.
1839, Mar. 29.	{ Orphans' Court Sales of Real Estate................	3	2 papers, 3 weeks once a week, one to be selected by petitioner.
1875, Mar. 18. / 1808, Mar. 26.	{ Partition—When Party not Found; Substance of Writ................	6	1 paper, 6 weeks once a week.
1835, April 11. / 1799, April 17.	" Sheriff's Sale of Land in one County when not taken at valuation................	2	90 days before sale and adv. as in other sheriff's sales.

ADVERTISEMENTS APPLICABLE TO PHILADELPHIA—(CONTINUED).

Date of Act.	Legal Intelligencer. Number of Insertions.	Other papers.
1799, April 17. Partition—When in Different Counties......		60 days before sale.
1836, Mar. 21. Partnership—Limited, Terms thereof, when registered, published......	6	2 papers, 6 weeks.
" Notice of Dissolution......	4	1 paper, 4 weeks once a week.
1853, April 18. Real Estate of Absentee unheard of for 7 years, or of Married Woman Abandoned for 2 years. Notice of Sale......	3	2 papers, 3 times each.
1832, Mar. 15. Register of Wills—Notice of Account Filed......	4	2 papers, 4 weeks once a week.
1836, June 16. 1860, Feb. 3. 1846, Mar. 11. {Sheriff's Sale of Real Estate. Also Tax Sales, January, April, July, October......	2	2 papers, 3 weeks, 3 times, and abstract once in German paper.
1846, Mar. 11. Taxes—Notice of Alias Writ of Scire Facias......		1 paper, 2 weeks twice a week.
1836, June 14. Trustees' Notice of Filing Account. Rule V......	4	2 papers, 4 weeks once a week.

PENNSYLVANIA LEGAL TIME-TABLE.

ARBITRATION.

1. VOLUNTARY.

The referee must be an attorney of the Supreme Court.

The submission must be filed with notice to the referee, who has twenty days to file acceptance with oath to act impartially. During this time, the referee shall appoint the time and place of meeting. Receives $10 per diem.

[PHILA. After notice of report filed, four days are allowed, excluding Sunday, to file exceptions, with affidavit, during which time execution shall not issue.]

2. COMPULSORY.—(Not applicable to Philadelphia.)

After narr. filed, either party may enter a rule of reference and notice of intention to choose arbitrators within thirty days. If the case be on the trial list, arbitration must be by mutual consent within thirty days before or during Ct. session, unless the case have been previously continued to next term. A certified copy of the rule must be served on opponent fifteen days before day of appointment.

Three to five arbitrators may be chosen, as the parties or Prothy. decide. If five, each party nominates two. If objected to, he nominates up to six to be selected from. Each party may nominate up to seven for an umpire. If all be objected to, Prothy. nominates up to seven. If

all these be objected to, he chooses five, and the parties strike out alternately until one be left. Same process where no selection of arbitrators by the parties.

If one party only be present, the Prothy. acts for the other. If no agreement as to meeting, the Prothy. chooses a day from ten to twenty days off. Party entering rule gives ten days' notice of meeting. Same notice to produce books and papers.

The award must be filed in seven days after it be given, or no compensation will be allowed to the arbitrator. It remains a lien for five years, and may be revived by sci. fa. Twenty days are allowed after the award be filed, in which to appeal, the witness costs being first paid.

ASSIGNMENT FOR CREDITORS.

The assignment must be recorded in the Recorder's office within thirty days from the date of its execution; and the inventory, with affidavit of assignee, must be filed in Com. Pleas Ct. office during the same time. The judge appoints two or more appraisers.

Where the Commonwealth has a lien, the assignee should give fifteen days' notice of the sale to the Aud. Gen. or the State Treas.

After one year, the court may cite the assignee to file his account. One year is allowed to appeal to the Supreme Court.

[PHILA. *Vide* Advertisements. File exceptions by the first day of the succeeding term, or the account will be confirmed.]

[*Vide* Auditors in Phila.]

2

ATTACHMENT OF VESSELS.

Attachments are granted by the Common Pleas Court, where no previous admiralty process has issued.

The Sheriff advertises in one paper, once a week, six times, the name, port and captain, the proposed sale, unless the vessel be discharged in three months, and also notice to file claim within three months. Sale will take place after three months' publication.

[ALLEGHENY. Lien for three months' wages and within sixty days after the wages become due. Other liens must be sued within two years after the cause of action accrues.]

ATTACHMENTS.

1. DOMESTIC, seldom resorted to.
2. FOREIGN, *vide* Foreign Att.
3. IN EXECUTION, *sur.* judgt. (vs. Garnishee), the writ is returnable the next return day or the next term. [PHILA. Interrogotaries with rule on garnishee to answer in twenty days as in Foreign Att. Forty-eight hours' notice of hearing of rule for judgment on the answers filed should be given. No narr. Rule to plead in eight days where the answers are unsatisfactory.] *Vide* Justices.
4. To ENFORCE DECREES in the Orphans' Court and in Equity.
5. Vs. SHERIFFS AND CONSTABLES for the non-return of process, etc.
6. FOR ALIMONY.

7. VS. NON-RESIDENTS' PROPERTY. *Vide* Justices.

8. VS. ATTORNEY, retaining money or papers.

9. VS. RECUSANT WITNESSES, subpœnaed by courts, arbitrators, auditors, coroner, registers and commissioners.

10. FOR CONTEMPT OF COURT, punishable by three months' imprisonment or less.

11. VS. ABSCONDING DFT. in the Orphans' Court.

12. VS. INSOLVENT BANKS.

13. VS. STOCK held in another's name.

14. UNDER ACT MARCH 17, 1869, where there has been fraudulent removal, concealment or assignment. Where no personal service, after the first day of the second term, proceed as in Foreign Att.

15. PHILA. VS. ABSCONDING DFT.'S PROPERTY in certain actions for personal torts.

AUDITORS IN PHILADELPHIA.

[*Vide* Advertisements.]

In Orph. Ct. auditors are appointed only by the request of all the parties. Except in Com. Pleas Ct. No. 3, auditors must have been 2 years at the bar.

Notice of auditor's intention to file report must be given in Com. Pleas Ct.; in Orph. Ct. 10 days' notice; in U. S. Ct. 2 weeks' notice—may be waived.

In Orph. Ct. report filed on Saturday, and if no exception, confirmed on second Saturday afterward. Confirmed in Com. Pleas Ct. *nisi* when filed; eight days thereafter to file exceptions. Distribution in twenty days if no writ of error be taken.

In Com. Pleas Ct. when issue desired, request must be made in writing of the auditor, with affidavit, within

forty-eight hours after the hearing is ended. The auditor must file his report within sixty days after his appointment, or it may be vacated, unless the time be enlarged.

BILL OF EXCEPTIONS, PHILADELPHIA.

The exceptions must be presented to the Judge within ten days after the verdict, who has twenty days thereafter to settle the same, on application, with forty-eight hours' notice to opponent and copy of exceptions served on him. In U. S. Ct. two weeks after verdict.

Exceptions to the Judge's charge must be taken before the jury retire.

Points to be charged upon must be handed the Judge at the close of the evidence, before the argument.

Where a nonsuit is ordered for insufficiency of evidence, or where a verdict with a point reserved, or a verdict reduced or set aside on a reserved point, ten days thereafter are allowed to file exceptions.

BILL OF PARTICULARS, PHILADELPHIA.

If not furnished in three months after demand, the court may order the common counts stricken off, and if no special counts exist, may nonsuit, on motion, where no good cause to the contrary be shown. In U. S. Ct. two months after demand, nonsuit on two weeks' notice.

BUILDING ASSOCIATIONS.

(A.) ACT APRIL 12, 1859.

Ten or more persons requisite as corporators. [PHILA. By Act February, 1853. Twelve persons.]

Capital stock $500,000. 2500 shares, $200 each. Charter granted by Com. Pleas Ct. [*Vide* Corporations. Act October 13, 1840.]

No periodical payment of over $2 per share.

Stockholder may withdraw on 30 days' notice, unless his stock be pledged for security. Entitled to amount paid and proportion of profits, less fines, etc.: Provided, except by consent of the directors, only one-half of the funds at any time can be so applied.

The highest bidder is entitled to a loan of $200 or more upon each share.

Where non-payment of instalments or interest by borrowing stockholders for six months, payment of the principal and interest, without deducting premium paid, may be enforced by legal proceedings on securities.

A borrower repaying a loan before the end of the eighth year of organization should be refunded one-eighth of the premium paid for each preceding year.

The association cannot hold over fifty acres of land, and must dispose of it in 10 years from organization.

(B.) ACT APRIL 29, 1874.

Five or more persons are required as corporators. Applications should be advertised in two papers of proper county for three weeks. Acknowledgment should be made before the Recorder by at least three original subscribers. The Governor, after examination, may direct incorporation. [*Vide* Corporations.]

Capital stock not over $1,000,000 maximum. Shares $500 each. If issued in series, no one series shall be over $500,000.

Withdrawing stockholder is entitled to interest after one year.

Highest bidder is entitled to a loan on each share of not more than the amount fixed by the charter for the full value of a share.

Other points of time are similar to the former act.

CAPIAS.

Plaintiff with notice has twenty days after return day to except to bail. [PHILA. With forty-eight hours' notice to Sheriff and defendant, bail examined and approved.] Bail must justify, or new bail be substituted and justify, within ten days after notice of exception. [PHILA. With forty-eight hours' notice of justification.]

[PHILA. Rules to show cause of action and discharge on common bail must be moved within six days from the return day of the process.]

Bail may surrender principal within fourteen days after the writ be served on them: 4 P. L. J. 360. Ten days if before justice.

Unencumbered freehold to the extent of £50 exempts from arrest. If in the county, defendant need only show existence and value. Plaintiff may show the encumbrance. If out of county, defendant must produce searches that it is clear of encumbrance: 2 M. 342.

CAPIAS, SPECIAL.

Where special capias is issued against a defendant about to remove, the Sheriff should make return within ten days.

The writ issues where the bail in any action assigns for creditors, or removes or is about to remove, upon affidavit, with rule and three days' notice to defendant, previous request having been made on the defendant to find additional bail.

CARRIERS, COMMISSION MERCHANTS AND FACTORS.

Where a lien exists against the owner or consignee for charges on goods, after sixty days from personal demand made, sell at auction sufficient to pay charges and costs. Notice of the sale should be published for three weeks in one paper, and six handbills posted.

Where an affidavit alleges that the owner and consignee are unknown, a Judge will authorize a sale upon such terms and notice as he thinks proper. If perishable property, a Justice may do it.

CERTIORARI.

To set the judgment of a justice aside, the writ from the Court must issue within twenty days after the judgment, and be served within five days thereafter. If, however, the record shows no jurisdiction, or the summons wrongly served, or of fraud, defendant not appear-

ing, the writ may issue within twenty days after the knowledge of the judgment by the defendant.

To set aside an execution, the writ must be served within twenty days after the execution was issued.

Six days' notice must be given to opponent of an intended motion to certiorari an indictment to the Supr. Ct. [*Vide* Error.]

[PHILA. Exceptions must be filed and record returned two days before the first day of argument. In landlord and tenant cases, a certiorari is a supersedeas, if issued within ten days from the date of the judgment.]

COLLATERAL INHERITANCE TAX.

Five per cent. charged on estates over $250. Penalty after one year. Discount allowed if the tax be paid within three months. Remainder men elect when to pay.

Executors, etc., have six months to give notice to Register, or one month thereafter after knowledge.

Thirty days after the appraisement to appeal to Orph. Ct.

Where Register cannot cite executor and heirs, he shall advertise in one paper once a week for four weeks.

Payment is presumed after twenty years.

COMMISSIONS FROM PHILADELPHIA COURTS.

Forty-eight hours' notice must be given of a rule for a commission to take testimony in other States. U. S. Cts. ten days' notice.

Interrogatories with the name of the commissioner must be filed and copy served fifteen days before the commission issues. In U. S. Ct. two weeks.

Counsel must not be present before the commissioner.

Exceptions may be filed within ten days after notice of return of commission. U. S. Ct. two weeks. Ten days thereafter to move for decision on exceptions, *aliter*, they may be argued at the trial.

[*Vide* Depositions.]

CONSTABLES.

A levy is a lien for twenty days, during which time the sale may take place after three bills posted. An alias execution may be subsequently issued, if the time expire.

Exemption should be claimed before the day of sale. Property of non-residents of State, also partnership property, cannot be exempted.

Where an execution is not returned, a justice or magistrate may summon the constable to appear within eight days. To sue a constable for an act done under a warrant of a justice, make a written demand on the constable for a certified copy of the warrant. If it be supplied,

3

the justice also becomes a defendant, thirty days' notice of intended suit being given him. If neglected for six days, the constable may be the sole defendant.

CORPORATIONS.

(A.) By Act Oct. 13, 1840, and amendments.

Where the charter is filed in Com. Pleas' Ct., advertise application in one paper three weeks. The Court will decree incorporation at the next term. Record charter in Recorder's office.

Advertise application to court for dissolution in two papers near the chief office.

In suing a company incorporated here, but having its office and officers outside the State, publish process in one paper, as the court may direct, six weeks before return day. Sue in the county where the business of the company had been transacted, or where the property or works are located.

Where foreign attachment, the clerk or agent must notify the principal in thirty days, or liable for treble damages.

Where effects are concealed, the court cites an officer to answer interrogatories on fifteen days' notice before return day, under penalty of attachment.

(B.) Under Act 29th April, 1874.

Corporation formed by five or more persons. Application should be advertised in two papers of proper county three weeks. Same notice for amendments. Acknowledgments of at least three original subscribers must be made before the Recorder of Deeds.

If the company be one not for profit, any law judge after examination may order incorporation. If for profit, the Governor, after examination, may approve and direct letters patent to be issued.

Stockholders in arrears for thirty days are barred from voting. They are liable individually to the amount of stock held by each for the work done and materials furnished to carry on the operations of the company.

In any action or bill in equity, the Plaintiff may include one or more of the stockholders. Suit therefor must be brought within six months after debt due. Execution shall first be made on corporation property in the county.

Thirty days' publication of notice of a meeting to issue preferred stock is requisite.

A corporation desirous of increasing its capital stock or indebtedness should publish the notice of an intended meeting once a week for sixty days, in one paper in the county of the chief office.

No one can vote on a share transferred within sixty days, nor by proxy executed within three months.

Thirty days are given to file return with Secretary of State.

(C.) In Actions vs. Stockholders.

Service of process in county like ordinary summons. If stockholder in another county, service by Sheriff of such county. If non-resident of State, publish notice of suit four times in a newspaper in original county, and also in the State where the stockholder lives, as the court may direct, and mail a copy of the publication to P. O. address, if it can be ascertained. Limitation of such action to six years after the debt was due or neglect of duty.

COSTS IN PHILADELPHIA.

Taxed with twenty-four hours' notice between 2 and 3 o'clock P. M. The party appealing has three days thereafter to file items objected to, and grounds therefor.

DECEDENTS' ESTATES.

No unsecured debt is a lien over five years after the decease of the debtor, unless the suit be duly prosecuted; or, if the debt be not due, a statement thereof be filed with the Prothy. Judgments are liens for five years after death, though not revived by sci. fa.

Devisees, heirs, etc., must apply within five years, unless incapacitated; then five years from the removal of the disability. In cases of personalty, the relatives of the intestate must claim within seven years.

Heirs accepting lands under an appraisement must give security to pay the other heirs within twelve months. After twenty years presumed paid.

Where a residuary estate is bound by a contingent or postponed legacy, the executor after one year may petition the Court to exempt a part of the real estate from the charge. One year to appeal, if the petition be granted. Executor every year thereafter shall report to the Court the condition of such retained property.

If plaintiff die, and no letters be taken out in this State within one year after his death have been suggested,

the suit abates and the Prothonotary makes entry, provided the Court directed notice served on executor or next of kin one month before.

Bequests or conveyances to charities, etc., made within one month of decedent's death are void.

Where an action to enforce a real contract of decedent, the contract must first be recorded, and notice given, allowing six weeks' time after the next succeeding Court for defendant to apply for leave to execute a deed.

If a sale in partition occur within two years after decedent's death, real estate in hands of purchaser is not liable for decedent's debts.

[PHILA. Notice to absent heirs, legatees, etc. *Vide* Advertisement.]

[*Vide* Collateral Inheritance Tax, Escheats, Executors and Administrators, Guardian, Limitations, Orph. Ct., Register, Widow.]

DEEDS.

Unless recorded within six months, deeds are void against subsequent bona fide purchasers and mortgagees, with prior record. Twelve months where the deed is executed outside of the State.

If land in two counties, file exemplification in second county.

The owner of land may demand, on six months' notice, the recording or delivery of title papers held by another, or the Court will grant decree.

Advertise lost deed three weeks before asking Court

for decree on testimony adduced. [PHILA. *Vide* Advertisement.]

The Recorder is liable for five years for false searches.

DEPOSITIONS IN PHILADELPHIA.

Depositions cannot be read, where the witness is a resident of the State and within forty miles, unless a subpœna be taken out (witness being in the State) and witness be subpœnaed, or not found after effort made.

Deposition of any witness taken on eight days' notice.

Depositions of ancient, infirm and going witnesses, and on rules to show cause on forty-eight hours' notice, Sunday excluded. For cause, Court may reduce this to six hours.

Except as to execution, form, etc., in ten days after notice of depositions filed. May be argued at trial or within ten days after exception filed.

[*Vide* Commissions.]

DIVORCE.

The libellant must have resided the last year in the State.

Where desertion is the cause, the action may be commenced six months after the act, but two years must expire before the divorce be decreed.

Marriage on false rumor of death of one absent two

years is not adultery. Six months is allowed after return for the absentee to claim his partner, or to ask the Court to dissolve the marriage.

Two years' sentence for a felony is a cause for divorce.

Either party may demand a jury trial before the examiner's report be filed.

The libel, endorsed by a Judge, must be filed thirty days before the next term.

The subpœna must be served personally fifteen days before.

Sheriff, with the written consent of a Judge, may deputize another Sheriff in any part of the United States to serve the subpœna personally and make return thereto.

[PHILA. Appearance should be entered by the respondent within ten days after return of writ. If not done in twenty days, proceedings *ex parte*, with twenty days' notice of the time and place of taking testimony. Rule to answer in thirty days. Interrogatories with notice of meeting, and names, residence and business of witnesses, must be served personally ten days before the meeting. Respondent at any time before the expiration of the ten days may file cross interrogatories. If respondent is not so served after personal service of the subpœna, publication should ensue. [*Vide* Advertisements.] Respondent may file interrogatories with ten days' notice to libellant to file cross interrogatories. Commission may issue with fifteen days' notice. Where proceedings are *ex parte*, post copy of interrogatories and notice in Prothonotary's office ten days before the examination of witnesses. Alimony pendente lite usually dates back to the return day of the writ. Personal service should be made of a rule for a decree one week

before the decree is granted, *aliter* publication. [*Vide* Advertisements.]

If subpœna be not served, issue alias to any subsequent term. If then no service, Sheriff on being ordered will publish to the next term the order of publication four weeks in one paper. Hence three distinct terms are required to perfect the entire process.

[PHILA. *Vide* Advertisements, also, as to rule for a decree. Post and file interrogatories with names, etc., in Prothonotary's office ten days before hearing.]

One year to appeal to Supr. Ct.

Libellant cannot testify unless the respondent have been personally served, or appears and defends.

EJECTMENT.

Entered in judgment index at outset.

No entry will arrest the Statute of Limitations unless ejectment be brought in one year thereafter.

Adverse possession for twenty-one years forces claimant to prove title under Statute of Limitations. Where plaintiff is under legal disability, the action must be brought within ten years from its removal, not in all to exceed thirty-one years. If statute pleaded, mesne profits prior to the last six years are barred.

Præcipe describes property. No narr. needed.

Defendant is not bound to appear until the second term, nor can there be judgment until then.

In vendor's action to enforce specific performance of

a contract of sale against an absent vendee of unoccupied land, publish rule to appear and plead sixty days before return day three times in one newspaper. Judgment then by default. Same rule in ejectment brought by claimants and mortgagees of such land, except actual notice must be given before trial and judgment.

In ejectment for unoccupied land sold for taxes, publish rule on absent defendant to appear and plead sixty days successively before return day in a weekly or daily paper. Judgment then by default.

Two verdicts for one party bar a third action between the same parties.

Where verdict and judgment, claimant may be ruled to commence another action within two years, or show cause. Where a nonsuit, or verdict for defendant, plaintiff may be ruled to sue out a writ of error in one year, or be for ever barred. Thereupon defendant may rule plaintiff to bring second action within one year, or show cause.

After a writ of hab. fac. poss. returned, Ct. may order alias within three years.

EQUITY.

Endorse on printed bill notice to defendant to appear within fourteen days or bill taken pro confesso.

Where a bill relates to real estate, on request, the Prothy. makes entry in judgment index at outset. Each party is entitled to ten copies of all the pleadings.

4

Injunction bills will be dismissed, unless in twenty days printed copies be filed and served.

Where a bill is taken pro confesso, the decree is absolute, unless set aside by the court within fourteen days after service of notice of such decree.

Rule to plead, answer or demur in thirty days. Demurrer and pleas must have an affidavit of not interposed for delay. If plaintiff does not set them down for argument in ten days after service thereof, defendant may do so on five days' notice.

Interrogatories and rule to answer within ten days may be filed by either party. Answers thereto may be compelled by attachment. Objections to an interrogatory may be argued on forty-eight hours' notice. Exception to a particular answer for insufficiency must be filed and served ten days before hearing. If sustained, defendant has ten days to file amended answer. Exceptions to an answer for scandal and impertinence must be filed in ten days after service of answer, and the case heard on forty-eight hours' notice. If allowed, ten days are given to perfect answer. Other exceptions to answer to interrogatories filed in twenty days after service.

Exceptions to answers to the bill must be filed and served ten days before hearing. If no exceptions to the answer, or if held sufficient, plaintiff should reply in ten days. May be ruled to do so.

Before replication filed, plaintiff without notice may have leave to amend the bill within twenty days.

Where a personal representative of decedent is to be joined, ten days' notice must be given him to appear.

Fifteen days' notice must be given of a commission. After notice by Prothy. of its return, ten days are allowed

to file exceptions; heard on forty-eight hours' notice. Depositions of ancient, etc., witnesses on reasonable notice.

Either party may rule opponent to close testimony in thirty days. Court may enlarge the time.

Party asking the appointment of a master should refer the case to him within ten days, *aliter* the other party may do it at the expense of the former. The master should give ten days' notice of filing his report. Exceptions thereto should be filed with him.

To place a case on the equity argument list, four days should intervene. [PHILA. Com. Pleas Ct. three days before calling of list with three days' notice to opponent.]

If no exceptions filed, report will be confirmed in twenty days after being filed.

Injunctions granted without previous notice will be dissolved, unless motion argued within five days after such notice given.

[PHILA. Rules expiring in July or August are deemed to expire on the same day in September.]

Counsel should frame decree and serve a copy with notice three days before submitting it to court, to give time to file exceptions.

[U. S. EQUITY CTS. IN PHILA. Printed rules exist, but have practically fallen into disuse.]

ERROR.

Where writ is issued for delay, Supreme Ct. assess six per cent. damages on judgment, $20 attorney fee and cost of printing. Limited to two years after the judgment, or decree obtained since April 1, 1874.

Murder and manslaughter, thirty days after sentence; hearing in Supreme Ct. should be within thirty days thereafter. Must be taken out within twenty days from a decree of distribution (in Com. Pleas Ct.) of proceeds of Sheriff's sale, or court will order the money paid.

Execution is stayed, where a writ of error is taken out within twenty-one days after the judgment. Supersedeas even after twenty-one days, where no actual levy made.

Twenty days' notice given to except to bail, with ten days thereafter to justify or nol. pros. by Prothy.

[*Nol. pros.* in Supreme Ct. Eastern District, where exceptions and record are not filed by first Monday in January in Philadelphia cases.]

Plaintiff by third day of term to which returnable must file specification of errors.

If no appearance when case called, proceed ex parte, ten days' notice having been given to defendant.

If writ of error be pending three years, plaintiff must be ready at next call and give thirty days' notice to defendant, or be non prossed.

[PHILA. Short causes will be heard in Supreme Ct. on Tuesday, and from country on Wednesdays. Paper-books must be served by plaintiff in error ten days before the argument, and by defendant three days before.]

Paper-books, in cases originating out of Philadelphia,

must be served by plaintiff in error ten days before the day appointed for the hearing, and by defendant three days before; but if the writ was taken thirty days before the day assigned, the paper-book of plaintiff must be served twenty days, and that of defendant five days before such appointed time.

[*Vide* Certiorari. Also Bill of Exceptions in Philadelphia.]

ESCHEATS.

Where the c. q. trust is unknown for seven years, his interest escheats. Twenty days' notice to claimants. Sheriff's sale after ten days' notice. Lands sold after seven years upon advertising one month in two papers.

Persons under disability have two years after its removal to claim personal property, and four years to claim real estate. Non-residents have five years from sale of goods, and seven from sale of land.

Commth. barred after twenty-one years. Informer receives one-third of personal property and one-fifth of real estate.

EXECUTIONS.

Issued within five years after judgment, or revival thereof or expiration of stay. On special verdict, demurrer or case stated, twenty-one days must elapse. Lien of test. fi. fa. continues five years.

In case of personal property, demand for exemption must be made before the day of sale. In real estate, before inquisition.

Six days' notice of sale of personal property by six handbills.

[PHILA. Where third party claims goods, interplead. *Vide* Feigned Issue.]

Rent for one year and wages for six months before sale to the extent of $200 have preference out of fund.

[PHILA. Executions levied on real estate acquired after judgment, may on application be docketed in judgment index and bind such real estate for five years.]

Stay of execution is computed from the return day of the writ. Refers to judgments upon actions *ex contractu*, except actions of debt and sci. fa. on judgments and mortgages. Not allowed where judgment entered on warrant of attorney. Six months on $200 or under. Nine months up to $500. Over $500, twelve months. [PHILA. If stay be entered after seven days from judgment, defendant must pay costs of execution unless execution executed.]

If fi. fa. has been issued within a year and a day, sci. fa. to revive unnecessary as to personal property.

[*Vide* Justices, Constables and Sheriff's Sales.]

EXECUTORS AND ADMINISTRATORS.

Publish notice of Letters Testamentary or of Administration in one paper once a week for six weeks. [PHILA.

Vide Advertisements.] No original letters granted after twenty-one years, except on order of the Court.

Except to bond within one year after the inventory be filed. Register notifies administrator or non-resident executor to appear within ten days. Neglect causes revocation.

Two appraisers are appointed. File inventory within thirty days and account within one year. If additional goods found, file inventory with Register in four months after discovery. Statement of goods sold at auction by executor or administrator should be filed in thirty days.

Notify corporation of a bequest within six months.

One year to make distribution, and to pay legacies and debts, except wages and expenses of illness and death. After six months, additional further distribution may be made.

Creditors should present claims within one year, if public notice be given.

Suit of administrator d. b. n. vs. predecessor must be stayed until judgment on the account, when it is filed twenty days before the term succeeding the return day of the writ.

The Court in which a suit of decedent is pending may issue sci. fa. forcing executors or administrators within twenty days to become parties, or show cause at the next term. If they are out of the State, by publication in a paper convenient to them, at option of the Court. The case will be continued one term.

If plaintiff die, and no letters be taken out in this State for one year, suit shall abate, one month's notice being given to next of kin.

Removal from State for one year, or no known resi-

dence, is a cause for the removal of executor or administrator.

Balances due by executors, etc., may be by transcripts made a lien in Com. Pleas Ct., and revived every five years. If paid, satisfaction must be entered within thirty days after notice, or $50 penalty, with damages sustained.

[*Vide* Decedent's Estates, Orph. Ct., and Register.]

FEIGNED ISSUES IN PHILADELPHIA.

Sheriff's interpleader is allowed where a third party claims the goods levied on under an execution. In this issue, the claimant becomes the plaintiff, and the original plaintiff the defendant.

The claimant must file narr., and give approved bond within fourteen days after the rule to interplead be made absolute.

FOREIGN ATTACHMENT.

Writ is returnable at the next term.

If real estate and no tenant, Sheriff shall advertise writ for six weeks in one paper, and file a description of property within five days after attaching. [PHILA. *Vide* Adver.]

Judgment against the defendant at third term for want of an appearance after narr. filed. Prothy. assesses damages.

Issue scire facias to garnishee to next term. [PHILA. Interrogatories filed and garnishee ruled to answer in twenty days. Plaintiff within three months after judg-

ment must issue sci. fa., or Court may on motion dissolve the attachment.]

Plaintiff either leaves property unsold for a year and a day, or enters security to restore the goods or their value, if defendant within a year and a day after execution disproves the debt.

Non-resisting garnishee is not liable for interest after attachment made.

Where one defendant is summoned and the other attached, and a verdict for defendant be given, the attachment will be dissolved, unless a writ of error be taken within a year and a day.

GROUND RENTS.

Two nihils are equivalent to service.

Alias writ covenant should be served on tenant, or posted on the premises ten days before return day, and publication be inserted in one or more papers, as the Court directs. [PHILA. *Vide* Adver.]

NOTE.—Under a special act, applicable only to Philadelphia, a statement, referring to the book and page of the record of a Ground Rent deed, or of its assignment, will suffice in lieu of filing a copy of the deed itself.

GUARANTEE.

A promise to pay the debt of another is not good where $20 or over, unless it be in writing.

5

ment must issue sci. fa., or Court may on motion dissolve the attachment.]

Plaintiff either leaves property unsold for a year and a day, or enters security to restore the goods or their value, if defendant within a year and a day after execution disproves the debt.

Non-resisting garnishee is not liable for interest after attachment made.

Where one defendant is summoned and the other attached, and a verdict for defendant be given, the attachment will be dissolved, unless a writ of error be taken within a year and a day.

GROUND RENTS.

Two nihils are equivalent to service.

Alias writ covenant should be served on tenant, or posted on the premises ten days before return day, and publication be inserted in one or more papers, as the Court directs. [PHILA. *Vide* Adver.]

File within two weeks after return day of the first summons a copy of the deed. Also file narr.

To obtain judgment on quarto die post, the alias writ must have issued ten days before the return day.

Twenty-one years is a limitation to the action, unless a clear acknowledgment.

GUARANTEE.

A promise to pay the debt of another is not good where $20 or over, unless it be in writing.

5

GUARDIAN.

Thirty days after property in possession is allowed to file inventory. Account should be filed every three years and when the ward arrives at age.

The Court will not appoint an exr. or admr. a guardian also. Father cannot appoint a testamentary guardian, when for one year before his death he wilfully neglected the child.

Foreign guardian must give thirty days' notice to resident gdn., exr. or admr. of his intended application for their discharge in his favor.

Ward at age of fourteen may change his guardian.

Where guardian applies to the Court for leave to sell real estate, he must give thirty days' notice of hearing to minor and his next of kin in the county.

HABEAS CORPUS.

Officer within three days must make return to writ, or may be attached. Ten days, where party lives from twenty to one hundred miles distant. Twenty days, where over one hundred miles. Judge has two days thereafter to take bail or discharge prisoner.

[PHILA. Hearing usually on Saturdays.]

Person not indicted at the next term shall be released on bail, where wilful delay by Commonwealth. If not indicted and tried the second term [PHILA. fourth month], unless by defendant's consent, defendant will be discharged.

A penalty exists for not delivering to prisoner or agent,

six hours after request, a copy of the warrant of commitment.

Two years' limitation for penalties under the hab. corp. act. If party be out of prison, the limitation dates from the offence, otherwise it dates from freedom.

INN-KEEPERS.

A lien exists on baggage for board not exceeding two weeks. After three months, justice may order constable to sell after ten days' posted notice in three places. Owner may redeem up to sale on paying debt and costs.

[ALLEGHENY. Wages may be attached for four weeks' board.]

INSOLVENTS.

Six months' residence in State or three months' confinement is requisite before application can be made for discharge.

[PHILA. *Vide* Adver. of notice to Creditors. Publication fifteen days at least before hearing, or personal notice may be given with proof filed three days before hearing.]

In certain judgments for torts, imprisonment for sixty days before discharge on final hearing. Where $15 or less, thirty days or less.

Trustees of an insolvent should give notice of appointment for four weeks in one paper. Make distribution within twelve months.

[PHILA. Prothy. gives notice of account filed. *Vide* Adver.]

Rent for one year preferred.

Court may exempt from execution for seven years on consent of a majority of creditors in number and value.

JUDGMENTS IN PHILADELPHIA (IN PART).

(1.) NOL. PROS. in Supreme Ct. where no exceptions in error, and no record filed by first Monday of January.

(2.) NON PROS. where no narr. filed after rule to declare in eight days. Time often enlarged on forty-eight hours' notice of motion. In Supreme Ct. entered where failure after notice to justify bail.

(3.) NONSUIT. Where case called and plaintiff is absent, or if present he fails to make out his case.

(4.) UPON VERDICT, after four days elapse, in which motions for a new trial and arrest of judgment may be made.

(5.) UPON DEMURRER. Leave is usually given to amend where the pleadings are defective.

(6.) NON OBSTANTE VEREDICTO.

(7.) UPON TWO NIHILS upon certain writs of sci. fa.

(8.) FOR WANT OF A PLEA. Where service of rule to plead in eight days. Time enlarged on forty-eight hours' notice of motion.

(9.) FOR WANT OF AN APPEARANCE. Where writ served and narr. filed before return day. If ten days' service before return day, judgment may be taken quarto die post. *Aliter* fourteen days after return day. In U. S. Cts. one week must elapse. Not applicable to ejectment, partitions and writs of sci. fa.

(10.) FOR WANT OF AN AFFIDAVIT OF DEFENCE. Where

plaintiff has filed such an instrument of writing as is required by Act March 28, 1835, or affidavit of loan or advance required by Act March 11, 1836, within one week after return day, or if filed the second week, has given forty-eight hours' written notice of his intention to apply for judgment in an original case, or where an appeal from a justice and no affidavit of defence to copy of claim filed in such time, judgment on motion on third Saturday after return day.

(11.) FOR WANT OF A SUFFICIENT AFFIDAVIT OF DEFENCE. Forty-eight hours' notice of hearing of rule for judgment.

JUDGMENTS.

Lien on real estate for five years. May be revived by sci. fa., which must be prosecuted to judgment in five years, or the lien of the original judgment is lost.

Where the judgment is paid, plaintiff must satisfy within eighty days after tender of charges, or maximum penalty of half of debt. [PHILA. Where judgment of ten years' standing has been paid or compromised and no satisfaction, Court may, on proof shown, order the Prothy. to satisfy after personal or published notice.]

JUSTICES OF THE PEACE AND MAGISTRATES.

Summons returnable in five to eight days, between hours named, with four days' service.

Where plaintiff is a non-resident of the State, or defendant is a non-resident of the county, short summons

may issue returnable in two to four days with two days' service.

Twenty days to enter stay or to appeal from judgment over $5.33, the day of judgment excluded. If the twentieth day fall on Sunday, Monday is in time. The time is extended where there has been a neglect of the justice, or where a rule to open judgment is pending.

If both parties assent to transfer case to referees from justice, no award unless appeal exceeds $20.

Stay may be entered even after twenty days, if no execution issued. The bail on appeal is for costs only, except in capias and suit for wages. Exrs., admrs. and gdns. need not give security.

Enter appeal in the court on or before the first day of the next term after it was taken. [PHILA. File appeal on or before the next return day after the judgment, by Act May 1, 1861, although the custom is to file the appeal before the next return day after the appeal was taken.]

No nonsuit except for want of an appearance.

Set-off under $100 must be presented or be for ever barred. May be done in Court on appeal. Where a judgment by default, the defendant having a set-off, may have a rehearing within thirty days, on proof of absence, sickness, etc.

Where depositions are to be taken out of the county file interrogatories, serving copy on opponent, who has four days to file cross interrogatories. Not filed where witness is in the county.

After five years, no execution unless sci. fa., or amicable confession.

Three months stay of execution on judgments of $20

or less; six months on $60 or less; over $60, nine months. No stay allowed in judgment for wages of manual labor.

Penalty of one-fourth of debt when, after 30 days' written notice of payment, plaintiff neglects to satisfy the judgment, unless in fifteen days after payment, any defendant forbid him by writing filed with justice.

Where capias and judgment, and sci. fa. against bail, ten days allowed to deliver up principal. Criminal returns to Q. S. Court made ten days before session of Court to which returnable, if recognizance have been given.

(A.) Attachments against garnishees returnable in four to eight days. Served like summons. File interrogatories by return day, to be answered in eight days. Wages and salary not attachable in hands of employer. Plaintiff, defendant or garnishee may appeal. Claim exemption before day of hearing.

(B.) Attachments on property for intent to defraud creditors, returnable in two to four days, with two days' service. If no service, issue summons, and if defendant not found, the justice will proceed in his absence. Defendant not served has thirty days after judgment to apply for a rehearing, with four to eight days' notice to opponent. Attachments are a lien for sixty days from the date when execution could issue. If appeal taken, lien continues sixty days from final judgment.

(C.) Upon affidavit and bond filed, attachment issues against property of non-resident of State, returnable in two to four days, with two days' service. If no personal service, issue summons, and the case will proceed whether he be found or not. No exemption allowed.

Thirty days' full written notice must be given to justice or magistrate of an intended suit for his official act, which suit must be brought within six months after the act or knowledge thereof by plaintiff.

Suit against surety of justice, in eight years from the date of the bond.

Against surety of magistrate, in six years from the time the action accrued.

LANDLORD AND TENANT.

Leases for more than three years must be in writing.

(A.) To RECOVER POSSESSION.

Where the tenancy is from year to year, give three months' notice to quit before the year expires. If disobeyed, issue summons returnable in four to eight days before justice or magistrate, who may give judgment of possession, with damages and costs, enforceable by constable. Ten days to appeal in bail absolute for rent and costs up to final judgment. [In Phila. the appeal is a supersedeas.]

Where a lease expires at a definite time, and also where ownership under Sheriff's deed, after three months' notice given to quit, a justice or magistrate shall issue writ to Sheriff to summon twelve freeholders to appear before the magistrate. Summon tenant also. Returnable in four days.

If the tenant allege the property to be claimed by another than plaintiff, summon such party to appear in

six days. Claimant may give bond to appeal to next Com. Pleas Ct.

Where the lease is lost or the date be unknown, the tenant must furnish to the landlord, in thirty days after written notice to him, the date such tenancy commenced. If he neglect, the landlord may give three months' notice thereafter to quit. If the tenant swears before the thirty days expire, that he cannot give the date, the landlord may give him six months' notice to quit.

Tenant in arrears, not having goods over amount exempted, may be notified between April 1st and September 1st to quit in fifteen days, and in thirty days during the remainder of the year. If he disobey, the magistrate summons him to appear in from three to eight days. Judgment of possession with costs, enforceable by constable, who has ten days to make return. Payment before execution stops proceedings. Five days after such judgment before execution issues [PHILA. Ten days.], in order to allow appeal, which is in bail absolute for rent and cost up to final judgment.

[PHILA. If tenant remove, leaving insufficient property for three months' rent, or refuse to give security therefor in five days after demand or to deliver possession, magistrate may summon lessee in five to eight days, and give judgment of possession, enforceable by constable. No writ of possession is allowed in any case until ten days expire, during which time certiorari may issue.]

(B.) DISTRESS.

Must be made in the daytime, but not on the day the rent falls due.

Holding a note or judgment does not bar distress.

Thirty days are allowed to follow goods clandestinely

removed, not in hands of bona fide purchaser without notice.

Landlord may remove the goods at once, or leave them on the premises under a watchman or with security. Must have tenant's consent to let goods remain more than five days after levy, or it is trespass. If last day falls on Sunday, Monday is in time to remove the goods.

If in five days after the day of the distress, the tenant does not replevy, the party distraining, aided by the Sheriff or constable, may appraise and after six days' notice sell the goods.

Landlord's claim for one year's rent is preferred out of the proceeds of any execution or of funds in assignee's hands. [*Vide* Replevin.]

[PHILA. AND ALLEGHENY. Thirty days to follow goods fraudulently removed before the rent is due. The landlord must apportion rent, and make oath that it will not affect bona fide purchasers.]

LIMITATIONS.

(A.) REAL ESTATE.

Entry on real estate barred after twenty-one years' adverse possession. [PHILA. forty years.] Thirty years is the extreme limit where legal disability. If proceedings abate, three years to recommence. Six years' quiet possession under Sheriff's deed bars objection to defects of process and execution.

Thirty years' continuous possession is evidence as between parties litigant that the Commonwealth title is divested. Where Commonwealth might have claimed

land held by a corporation, twenty-one years' possession without inquisition by Commonwealth renders such title indefeasible in purchaser. Twenty-one years after death of intestate for Commonwealth to claim escheat.

Ground rents, annuities or rents charge are presumed released or extinguished, unless claimed or acknowledged within twenty-one years.

Five years to sue for specific performance of real contract or damages therefor, or to enforce equity of redemption after re-entry for conditions broken or on implied and resulting trusts, except where concealed fraud, or in trusts where lands are purchased by attorneys.

In ejectment, sue within one year after entry.

Judgments and balances due by exrs. entered in Com. Pleas Ct. are liens on real estate for five years only, unless revived by sci. fa.

Probate of will is conclusive as to real estate, unless contested in five years.

Taxes are a lien for five years.

Six months to file municipal claims and mechanics' liens.

Trespass six years.

(B.) Personal.

Detinue, trover, replevin for goods and cattle, action upon account and upon the case other than merchants' accounts with merchants, factors or servants, debt, grounded on lending or contract without specialty, or debt for arrearages of rent six years.

Running or mutual accounts, where some items are within six years, bar the statute. Runs from the discovery of fraud. Clear acknowledgment made to plaintiff or agent within six years takes the case out of the statute. Not so

if made by executor, though he need not plead statute. Nor by defendant's attorney, nor by one partner after the dissolution of firm. Writ issued within six years after original bars statute.

A claim against decedent's estate is not barred where six years expire after the death and before the settlement of the estate, unless an action against personal representative. Where legal disability, date from removal.

In debt on bond, sci. fa. on judgment and collateral inheritance tax, payment is presumed after twenty years.

Five years against railroad for use of land, or three years after road operated, and two years for penalties.

Relatives of intestate decedent are barred as to claim for personalty in seven years.

Usurious interest recoverable within six months from date of payment of debt.

Illegal fees of officers, six months.

Penalties under habeas corpus Act, two years.

Trespass as to person, assault, battery, menace or imprisonment, two years.

Slander and libel, one year.

Treason, arson, sodomy, robbery, burglary, perjury, forgery, counterfeiting and uttering such paper, five years. All other crimes two years after their commission.

Not applicable to absentee from State.

Six years where misdemeanor committed by officer of corporation.

After reversal or arrest of judgment, where plaintiff gained the case originally, one year is allowed to recommence.

Two years for error, or certiorari to the Supr. Ct.

LIVERY-STABLE MEN.

Lien exists on a horse for its keep.

If the owner does not pay a bill of $30 or over in fifteen days after demand, or in case of removal, within ten days after notice of amount due, and demand left at usual place of abode, the horse may be sold at public sale.

LUNACY.

Three months after the return is allowed to file traverse of inquisition.

Committee should file inventory of personal estate, with a statement of the real estate of the lunatic, within forty days after the trust be assumed. An additional inventory should be filed in forty days after any new discovery.

Where a party in prison under a civil action is reported insane by a justice to a Judge, the latter gives ten to twenty days' notice of hearing for his discharge by publication, and one week's notice to creditors.

Where a decree affects real estate, file a certified copy with the Recorder within six months.

MECHANICS' LIENS.

Must set forth name of claimant, of reputed owner and of contractor or builder, if contract made with the latter, amount due, nature of work or kind of materials, time, locality, size and number of stories, or other description to identify it. Usual to attach bill of items.

Claims against two or more adjacent buildings should be apportioned.

Unless buildings are on one lot, file distinct claims.

Claim filed within six months after work done or material furnished to each house. May count from last item.

No sci. fa. shall issue within fifteen days of the succeeding return day.

If defendant be not found, serve writ on tenant, *aliter* post on door of building.

Other lien claimants may become parties to the action by suggestion.

Lien expires in five years, unless revived by sci. fa.

Claimant may be required to file affidavit of the amount actually due.

May be ruled to sue out sci. fa. to next return day, or the lien be stricken off. Defendant may give bond and have lien stricken off.

On payment, 60 days after request are allowed to satisfy, or penalty of one-half the claim or less.

In half the State a claim for $20 or over may be filed for alterations, additions or repairs to old houses, but in Phila. such claim must be for more than $50, and the

debt have been contracted by the owner, or by the tenant with written consent of the owner, a copy of which assent must be filed with the claim.

MORTGAGES.

Purchase money mortgages recorded within sixty days are a lien from the date of execution. Other mortgages become a lien when recorded.

If two mortgages be recorded the same day, the first one brought to the recorder has a priority. If a judgment and a mortgage, they take pro rata.

Sci. fa. may issue one year after the mortgage be due, unless, as is usually the case, there be a contrary proviso. If no service, alias writ and judgment on two nihils. Judgment by default for want of an appearance may be taken, where service and no appearance on quarto die post, and where writ served ten days before return day.

Narr. unnecessary, description with reference to record being embodied in præcipe. No stay of execution.

Judgment need not be revived after five years.

Sell under a levari facias.

SATISFACTION.

If a mortgage be not satisfied within three months after payment and request, penalty not beyond amount of mortgage. If payment by instalments, on request, receipt on record within sixty days, or penalty of amount of instalment or less.

Where holder dies after payment, or removes or con-

tinue absent from State two years, neglecting to enter satisfaction, petition court to order Sheriff to notify representative in the county. If none, advertise once a week four times in one paper to mortgagee to appear at the next term. [PHILA. *Vide* Adver. also as to lost mortgages.]

Where the mortgage is forged, Court will order Sheriff to notify mortgagee or representative. If not found, advertise once a week in two papers for eight weeks before next term. The Court in default of defence will then order satisfaction.

MUNICIPAL CLAIMS IN PHILADELPHIA.

Must be filed within six months after the work was done or the materials furnished to constitute a lien. Entered in locality index of court. Expires in five years, unless revived by sci. fa.

Defendant may notify plaintiff or city solicitor to issue sci. fa. to next return day, fifteen days distant. If not done, Court may strike claim from record. Before writ. issues, city solicitor must search for owner, and if found, give him ten days' notice. If out of city, fifteen days' notice by mail, of which sworn proof must be given before judgment.

Sci. fa. published by Sheriff twice a week for two weeks in one daily paper, with posting on premises.

Sales January, April, July, October.

Equity of redemption for two years after acknowledgment of Sheriff's deed, on payment of twenty per cent.

on amount of bid. Property of minor not sold until two years after he becomes of age.

[*Vide* Taxes.]

NEW TRIALS IN PHILADELPHIA.

Motions for new trials, or in arrest of judgment, or to take off nonsuit, must be made and reasons assigned therefor in writing, within four days after the verdict. The day of verdict is excluded, also Sunday, where it is the first or fourth day thereafter. This, too, even if points reserved. Copy of reasons filed must be served on the Judge.

If counsel show a prima facie case when reached on the new trial motion list, his motion will be transferred to the argument list, when opposing counsel will be heard.

ORPHANS' COURT.

Citation to appear is returnable in not less than ten days from the date of the application. If party and surety are not found, issue alias. Publication in two or more papers, as the Court directs, and the Court makes decree. If defendant within five years and one year after notice appear and pay costs, he may be heard.

Within five years after final decree confirming account of exr., etc., for errors in record, the Court will grant rehearing, with right of appeal for one year.

Appeal from final decree of Orph. Ct. to Supr. Ct. in

7

three years. Shall not stay execution of a final decree, unless notice and security within twenty days after the decree was made.

Confirmation of appraisement of real estate is conclusive, unless appeal to Supr. Ct. in three months.

[PHILA. Widows' appraisement. *Vide* Adver. Exceptions presented second Saturday after notice expires.]

Notice should be given for application for order of sale of real estate devised; also, twenty days' notice of sale by posting and publication in one paper. [PHILA. *Vide* Adver.] Where exr., etc., dies after sale, and no successor be appointed in three months, Court may direct the clerk to execute a deed. So also where the exr., etc., neglect for eighty days after notice to execute or deliver the deed.

Upon non-resident executor, etc., producing exemplification of record, the Court, with thirty days' notice, may discharge resident executor, guardian, etc.

After twenty years from date of administrator's bond, payment is presumed. Where additional bond by order of Court, seven years gives presumption of payment.

Transcripts of amounts found due by auditor may be filed in Com. Pleas Ct.

[*Vide* Decedent's Estate, Guardian, Register, Widow.]

[PHILA. Exceptions to the settlement of an account or to a decree of distribution filed with copy should be handed to the auditing Judge by third Saturday after adjudication filed. Clerk on order of Court approves security of guardian or trustee under $2000. Where real estate is valued over $1000, applications are referred to a master or examiner. Preliminary injunctions argued in five days, unless special order. Subpœnas taken out

five days before day of auditing account.] [*Vide* Depositions, Commissions, Advertisements and Auditors.]

[PHILA. Auditors are only appointed when all parties request. No lien on report for fee, but may attach therefor. Audit lists. *Vide* Advertisements.]

PARTITION.

The writ is returnable at the next term.

Service of the summons and notice of the inquisition should be made on resident defendants in the county twenty days before the return day, or the day of taking the inquisition. *Aliter*, publish the substance of the writ in a paper once a week for six weeks prior to the return day.

A party taking at the valuation may enter security to pay the other heirs their proportions in one year. If not so taken, the Court will order sale, with advertisement, twenty days before the sale. If the lands are in different counties, sixty days' notice must be given. Defendants before return day may ask the plaintiff's part only to be set out.

If the sale occur two years after decedent's death, the real estate is not liable in the hands of a purchaser for the debts of the decedent.

If the land be in different counties, file exemplifications of record of inquest in all. If in adjoining counties, record exemplifications with Sheriff's deed in six months after execution in such county.

After ten days' public notice of a writ executed and

the inquest of partition be returned, final judgment may
be taken.   One year thereafter to present matter in bar
of partition.

PARTY WALLS IN PHILADELPHIA.

One month is allowed to appeal from the decisions of
surveyors or regulators.   Persons under disability may
appeal within three years after the disability be removed,
or one year after notice.

Building inspectors may examine dangerous walls on
forty-eight hours' notice to owner or agent.   Owner has
three days to appeal to the board of surveys.

PLEADINGS IN PHILADELPHIA.

Rules to declare or plead in eight days.   U. S. Court,
two weeks' time ; extended by Court on forty-eight
hours' notice of application.   Four days after narr.
served, is the time allowed to file dilatory plea.

Notice of set-off must be given ten days before the
first day of the period in which the cause is down
for trial.

Under plea of payment in an action on bond or other
specialty, defendant must give thirty days' notice before
trial, of the matter to be offered in avoidance.

PRACTICE.

(Altered in Philadelphia, Allegheny and many other counties.)

In actions in Court on a verbal promise, book account, note, bond or bill, the plaintiff should file a statement or demand by the third day of the term to which the action is returnable. Defendant at least twenty days before the next term should file his statement of set-off, if he has any, or of the amount due the plaintiff. Judgment by default where the defendant does not appear and defend, or of nonsuit where the plaintiff does not appear on the third day of the next term after return day if the term be for one week, or on the second Monday of the term if it is to continue two weeks. If there be a defence, go to a jury.

PROCESS.

Writs are returnable to the first day of the next term, or in many counties to the first Monday of the next month, at the plaintiff's option.

Except in Phila. and Allegheny, ten days must intervene between the day on which a summons is issued and the return day; and if no such interval, the summons may be returnable on the next day preceding the last day of the term, or the first day of the succeeding term.

QUO WARRANTO.

Writ is returnable at discretion of Judge. Must be served ten days before the return day, like a summons. Judgment may be taken by default.

RAILROADS.

~~' ~~ ~~l ~~ ~~f ~~ ~~———— of land or three~~

NOTE.—The Section on Railroads is probably annulled by Section 21, Article III., of the Constitution of 1874.

At this date, May, 1875, the Supreme Court has given emphasis to that Section, as to one point at least, in Central Railway of N. J. *v.* Cook, reported in *Weekly Notes* and *Legal Intel.*, April, 1875.

~~REAL ESTATE.~~

Where an owner has been absent and unheard of for seven years, the law presumes him dead, or where a married woman owns real estate and her husband has abandoned her for two years, the Court may order a sale, which may be partly on credit. Advertise by twenty handbills and in two papers, three times in each. The Court may authorize a private sale. Before the decree be carried into effect, twenty days is allowed from its entry to appeal.

Trusts for the accumulation of rents, interests, etc., shall not extend over the life of the grantor, and twenty-one years thereafter, except for charities, etc.

QUO WARRANTO.

Writ is returnable at discretion of Judge. Must be served ten days before the return day, like a summons. Judgment may be taken by default.

RAILROADS.

Five years to be sued for occupancy of land, or three years therefor after the road is in operation. Two years to be sued for penalties, and one year for damages for injuries received through negligence.

No limit as to amount of damages except when death results from injuries received.

REAL ESTATE.

Where an owner has been absent and unheard of for seven years, the law presumes him dead, or where a married woman owns real estate and her husband has abandoned her for two years, the Court may order a sale, which may be partly on credit. Advertise by twenty handbills and in two papers, three times in each. The Court may authorize a private sale. Before the decree be carried into effect, twenty days is allowed from its entry to appeal.

Trusts for the accumulation of rents, interests, etc., shall not extend over the life of the grantor, and twenty-one years thereafter, except for charities, etc.

REGISTER OF WILLS.

Where a will contains a legacy or a bequest to a public corporation, the register must notify the officers by letter within six months.

The register may file his bill of costs and fees in any matter in the Com. Pleas Ct. after thirty days from the time they were due, and issue execution in the name of the Commonwealth.

Thirty days having expired after the account of an exr. or admr. has been filed, the register shall send certified copy to the Orph. Ct., and advertise in two papers four weeks, also post in seven places. [PHILA. *Vide* Adver.]

May cite a party holding a will to deposit it for probate within fifteen days, and cite witnesses in the county or within thirty miles in the State to appear at a day not less than five days distant.

Nuncupative wills cannot be probated until fourteen days after the death of the party. Testimony thereon will not be admitted after six months, unless committed to writing by the witness within six days.

Appeals from Register to Orph. Ct. three years; to Supr. Ct. one year, where over $150 is involved.

REPLEVIN.

Limitation six years. Two kinds.

(1.) In the detinet, where the defendant in replevin retains possession by filing claim property bond, which cannot be done in rent cases.

(2.) In the detinuit, where the plaintiff obtains the goods. In the latter case the defendant usually rules the plaintiff to declare [PHILA. in eight days], then defendant may file avowry and cognizance, and rule plaintiff to plead. Pleas are non cepit, no rent in arrear, Stat. of limit., property or justification and avowry or cognizance, or in abatement, that property is in third person.

[*Vide* Landlord and Tenant.]

SHERIFF.

The Court may enforce the return of writs and payment of money by attachments at any time within two years after the Sheriff's term expires. Suits against Sheriffs for excessive fees must be brought within six months. Other suits on his bond within five years after the recognizance was given.

SHERIFF'S SALES.

The Sheriff should give five days' notice of holding inquisition personally or by handbills. [PHILA. Held on Friday before return day.] If, on proof shown, he find seven years' rent will pay the debt and costs, the plaintiff can obtain the land under a writ of liberari facias, and collect the rents until his judgment be paid, or until the land be sold under another execution. May be waived by the plaintiff, and the defendant allowed to retain. The Sheriff has ten days thereafter to notify the defendant, who accepts or rejects in writing in thirty days. If he assent and is in default of payment of any semi-annual instalment in thirty days, the plaintiff may issue a writ of vend. ex.

In executions upon life estates, where the defendant or occupant gives the plaintiff three days' notice before inquisition, the Sheriff appraises annual value, and gives thirty days to elect to pay such value in semi-annual instalments. *Aliter*, act as if a fee simple, giving ten days' notice of application for a writ of vend. ex.

The Sheriff's sale must be made on or before the return day, or within six days thereafter. Bills should be posted ten days before the sale.

Publish sale of real estate in two papers, one in English and the other in German, if one in the county, once a week for three weeks. [PHILA. *Vide* Advertisements.]

Deeds are acknowledged on the first Monday of term,

s

or upon any Saturday in open court.   One week after the return day must expire.

Where lien creditors purchase, the return shall be read in Court on the Saturday succeeding the filing of the return, and exceptions to the purchaser's right to the proceeds of the sale may be filed with the Prothy. by the next Wednesday, and the purchaser be ruled to show cause why the sale should not be set aside, returnable the next Saturday.   If the Court believe the lien creditor is not entitled, the rule will be made absolute, and unless the purchaser within ten days after the decision pay the purchase money to the Sheriff, the Court may grant an issue or refer to an auditor.

[As to the process of obtaining possession after sale, *vide* Justices and Landlord and Tenant.   Also *vide* Executions and Partition.]

TAXES IN PHILADELPHIA.

Registered taxes are a lien for five years from January 1 of the year after they are due.   If a suit be pressed thereon, the lien dates from the judgment.

Suit may be sci. fa. or by summons, but is almost invariably by sci. fa.   Act March 11, 1846, orders in case of sci. fa. that there shall be posting on premises and advertisement twice a week for two weeks in one paper before the return day.

If the land does not bring enough to pay taxes, sale stayed, unless the city purchase.   Property then not

irredeemable unless six months' previous notice be published by the city solicitor, after which he may sell with same notice as in Orph. Ct. sales.

Equity of redemption within two years from the acknowledgment of Sheriff's deed.

Tax sales by the Sheriff, January, April, July, October. [*Vide* Municipal Claims.]

TRIAL BY JURY.

Parties not acting in a fiduciary capacity may waive a jury trial, and by agreement filed submit the decision to the Court, which decision shall be in writing and filed within sixty days. If no exception be filed in thirty days after notice, judgment shall be entered.

Judges must see that all cases shall be reached and have a fair opportunity for trial within one year after they were commenced.

[PHILA. Causes must be at issue before the venire goes out, which is thirty days before the period.

Causes transferred to another term must be, by written consent of both parties, filed three weeks before the period.

When by mistake of the clerk a case is omitted from the trial list, either party may order it on with ten days' notice before the day marked for trial.

TRUSTEES.

In trusts for life or marriage, trustee at the end of three years may be cited to file account on thirty days' notice. When filed, the Court may cite parties in interest to appear on a day between twenty and thirty days thereafter, to show cause why the trustee should not be discharged.

Appeal to the Supr. Ct. from the Com. Pleas Ct. in three years.

[PHILA. *Vide* Advertisements.]

UNSEATED LANDS.

Sixty days' notice of sale for taxes in two papers. Sale to commence the second Monday of June. Purchaser, after paying taxes and costs, gives surplus bond to county treasurer for balance. The bond, when entered, is a judgment for five years, upon which, after three months from entry, execution may issue. Two years to redeem, with twenty-five per cent. additional. Actions for recovery barred after five years from sale, or two years from removal of disability. [*Vide* Ejectment, as to unoccupied land.]

If lands are purchased by county commissioner, not

bringing enough to pay taxes, five years are allowed to redeem. Then the commissioner sells after thirty days' notice in county paper and six posters.

VIEWERS.

Appeals from assessments of damages made by viewers to Com. Pleas Ct. within thirty days after ascertainment of them on the filing of a report thereon.

WAGES.

Lien on money in Sheriff's hands for labor to the extent of $200 done within six months, if claimed by notice to Sheriff before sale.

Appeals from judgments before justice for wages must be for debt as well as costs.

Orders on employers from operatives ten days before wages due to pay contributions to charitable institutions are a lien thereon.

Cannot be attached for debt. [Except in Allegheny. *Vide* Innkeepers.]

WARRANT OF ARREST IN CIVIL ACTIONS.

[Seldom resorted to in Philadelphia.]

Defendant released on giving security to pay debt in sixty days, if time for stay has expired, or when stay

shall expire, if over sixty days distant. Same rule where a judgment has not been obtained.

Where allegation of intended fraudulent removal, a bond may be given not to remove or sell property until the debt be paid, or until thirty days after the final judgment in the suit. The defendant will be released on giving security that within thirty days he will apply for the benefit of the insolvent law.

Thirty days shall intervene between the time of presenting this petition and the time of hearing the same.

WASTE.

Remainder men must give five days' notice to tenant in possession before estrepment issues.

WIDOW.

One year to elect to take under will or dower, with knowledge on her part of the estate. Where intestacy, Court within one year may order inquest to find her interest in her husband's real estate. [PHILA. *Vide* Advert. as to claim for $300 appraisement.]

Where she claims out of real estate worth less than $600, Orph. Ct. may set it apart for her, and give her one year to pay appraised excess over $300.

If one year expire after the representative of decedent obtains his real estate and no partition have been made, the widow may ask the Court to award inquest.

WITNESSES IN PHILADELPHIA.

Take subpœna out five days before the day assigned for trial, or the action will not be continued for the absence of the party, if he were at his residence in the mean time.

Apply for attachment before 11 o'clock on the day fixed for trial, unless witness was in attendance and left without leave.